THE

CRICKET

LOVER'S
COMPANION

THE CRICKET LOVER'S COMPANION

Copyright © Summersdale Publishers Ltd, 2011

Text compiled and written by Oli Broom

Illustrations by Ian Baker

Summersdale Publishers Ltd
46 West Street
Chichester
West Sussex
PO19 1RP
UK

www.summersdale.com

Printed and bound by CPI Group (UK) Ltd, Croydon, CR0 4YY

ISBN: 978-1-84953-174-0

THE
CRICKET

LOVER'S
COMPANION

Richard Benson

Illustrations by Ian Baker

summersdale

CONTENTS

INTRODUCTION

I tend to believe that cricket is
the greatest thing that God ever
created on earth.

Harold Pinter

The origin of cricket is shrouded in mystery, but what is certain is that for at least 400 years the game, in a variety of formats, has captured the imagination of millions. What began as a rural game played by peasant children in medieval England has become one of the most widely followed sports in the world, a multi-million-dollar industry scrutinised by the media and with a global audience of billions.

With its quirks, nuances and traditions, cricket is a game said to be the epitome of Englishness, yet much of the rest of the world has now taken to it. The shortest games last for twenty overs each side, while Test matches can continue for five days, with lunch and tea breaks taken once daily. Cricket provides a narrative that can shape a summer, and this is possibly at the heart of its appeal. It is a game of skill, endurance and patience.

This miscellany, for anyone who has ever enjoyed cricket at any level, is full of stories from the depths of cricket's history, inspiring and amusing quotes from some of its most colourful characters and trivia to impress your friends with! This book is intended to remind you why you love cricket.

Cricket is first and foremost a
dramatic spectacle. It belongs
with theatre, ballet, opera
and dance.

C. L. R. James, *Beyond a Boundary*, 1963

The very word 'cricket' has become
a synonym for all that is true and
honest. To say 'that is not cricket'
implies something underhand,
something not in keeping with the
best ideals.

Sir Pelham Warner

THE ORIGINS OF CRICKET

The instinct to throw and to hit
is the basis of man's primitive
armoury.

H. S. Altham, *A History of Cricket, From the
Beginnings to the First World War*

Cricket probably began after the Roman Empire and almost certainly before the Normans invaded England. Research points towards a game that was played as a pastime, whereby one player throws an object (a small piece of rounded wood, stone or wool) at another who hits the object (with a stick, or club).

There is no evidence to tell us when this field game became one where the hitter defended a target from the missile, or when points were awarded for the distance the object was hit. Similarly, the evolution of cricket into a team game, from one involving only two players, is uncertain.

The game's genesis has been attributed variously to landed gentry, cloth-workers, peasant shepherds and iron workers. Most of these theories have a solid basis, although none is able to post enough evidence. What is agreed is that by Tudor times cricket had evolved far enough that it can be recognised as the game played today.

CRICKET TIMELINE

1550: evidence of cricket being played in Guildford, Surrey.

1598: cricket mentioned in Florio's Italian-English dictionary.

1676: first reference to cricket being played abroad, by British residents in Aleppo, Syria.

1709: first recorded inter-county match: Kent v Surrey.

1744: publication of the first known version of the Laws of Cricket, issued by the London Club, formalising the pitch as 22 yards long.

1787: first match at Thomas Lord's first ground in Dorset Square, Marylebone played between the White Conduit Club and Middlesex. Marylebone Cricket Club (MCC) formed by members of the White Conduit Club.

1844: first official international match: Canada v United States.

1873: first regulations restricting county qualifications, often regarded as the official start of the County Championship.

1877: first Test match: Australia beat England by 45 runs in Melbourne.

1889: County Championship officially constituted.

As there is nothing in the whole range of poetry or prose with which to point a parallel, it must be allowed that beside a perfectly timed boundary hit, on a hard ground, from fast bowling, all other delights of this life are as nothingness.

J. C. Snaith, *Willow the King*, 1899

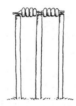

Cricket has been played pretty solidly in this country, and indeed throughout the Empire ever since the Norman Conquest, except perhaps during the Dark Ages, when bad light stopped play.

Ralph Wotherspoon and L. N. Jackson,
Some Sports and Pastimes of the English, 1937

IT'S A FUNNY OLD GAME

In November 1969, John Inverarity, playing in an Australian inter-state match, was clean bowled by a ball which had hit a bird flying over the pitch and had bounced on to the stumps. The umpire gave him 'not out'.

In the sixth Test between England and Australia at Adelaide in 1971, a shot by Keith Stackpole hit a seagull, slowing the ball down and losing him two runs.

In 1972, Jeff Thomson, one of the fastest bowlers ever to play Test cricket, attempted to get into the *Guinness Book of Records* by beating the egg-throwing record. He failed, because he couldn't work out a method by which eggs thrown over a long distance would remain intact when they landed in his hands.

FAMOUS CRICKETER: W. G. GRACE

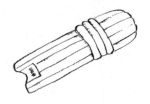

First-class: 54,211 runs (39.45), 2,809 wickets (18.14) and 876 catches

Tests (22): 1,098 runs (32.29), 9 wickets (26.22) and 39 catches

No monument, no portrait, no book can adequately represent either the vitality of W. G. or his superb skill in the game he loved.

Lord Hawke

Dr William Gilbert Grace (1848–1915) is arguably the most famous cricketer there has ever been, and remains the very embodiment of English cricket. Like many Victorian sportsmen, he did not specialise as a young man, and was adept at other sports in his youth, winning the 440 yards hurdling title at the National Olympic Games at Crystal Palace in 1866. He later went on to become a doctor in his home city of Bristol, employing two locums during the cricket season so he could fulfil his duties on the pitch.

But before his medical career took over, Grace could have walked into any cricket side in the world. Having made his first-class debut for Gloucestershire in 1865 at the tender age of seventeen, he went on to become the greatest batsman in England for the next twenty years. He is widely regarded as the inventor of modern batting, and is certainly its greatest early exponent, at least until the arrival on the scene of Ranjitsinhji (more of whom later) in the mid 1890s. Aged twenty, he became the first player in modern cricket to score two hundreds in a game and he was the first player to score 2,000 runs in a season, making 2,739.

Grace's skill, competitiveness and instantly recognizable beard made him one of the most popular figures in Victorian England. At a time when access to rail travel was improving, crowds flocked to see England's greatest batsman playing matches all over the country. They loved a hero, and Grace was a public figure who embodied self-confidence, hard work and achievement, three characteristics that defined Victorian England.

Although Grace worked hard at his game, he insisted that cricket must also be enjoyable and even admitted that his family all played in a 'noisy and boisterous' manner. He was noted for being noisy and boisterous on the field throughout his career, and was extremely competitive, always playing to win.

However, his skill as a cricketer and popularity with the Victorian public are in stark contrast to the occasional scrapes and controversies that punctuated his career. On one famous occasion, Grace was bowled, and the bail fell to the floor. He simply replaced the bail and told the umpire, "Twas the wind which took thy bail off, good sir.' The umpire replied, 'Indeed, doctor, and let us hope thy wind helps the good doctor on thy journey back to the pavilion.'

Although his sportsmanship never harmed his relations with followers of the game, it was because of this trait, and his own insistence on his rights as a 'great' cricketer, that Grace did not enjoy good relations with most Australians he came across. Joe Darling, touring England for the first time in 1896, said: 'We were all told not to trust the Old Man as he was out to win every time and was a great bluffer'.

Not all Australians felt the same though. Grace had a fan in former Australian captain, and hero of the first Test played in England, Billy Murdoch: 'What do I think of W.G.? Why, I have never seen his like and never shall. I tell you my opinion, which is that W.G. should never be put underground. When he dies his body ought to be embalmed and permanently exhibited in the British Museum as "the colossal cricketer of all time".'

Even in England, although hugely popular, Grace was the subject of sportsmanship discussion. His good friend Lord Harris agreed that 'his gamesmanship added to the fund of stories about him'.

Personally, W. G. struck me as the most natural and unspoilt of men. Whenever and wherever one met him he was always the same. There was not the smallest trace of affectation about him. If anything annoyed him he was quick to show anger, but his little outbursts were soon over. One word I will add. No man who ever won such worldwide fame could have been more modest in speaking of his own doings.

Sydney Pardon writing Grace's obituary notice in the 1916 edition of *Wisden* (or *Wisden Cricketers' Almanack*), the so-called 'bible' of cricket, first published in 1864 by Sussex cricketer John Wisden and still published annually

Those who knew him will never look at the classic sward of Lord's without an occasional vision of the great cricketer. He was, and will remain, the very impersonation of cricket, redolent of fresh air, of good humour, of conflict without malice, of chivalrous strife, of keenness for victory by fair means, and utter detestation of all that was foul. Few men have done more for the generation in which he lived, and his influence was none the less because he was a spontaneous and utterly unconscious one.

Arthur Conan Doyle on W.G. Grace's death in October 1915

CRICKET JARGON

Long ago I discovered there was more to life than cricket: and more to cricket than runs and wickets.

David Foot, *Cricket's Unholy Trinity*

T20 – Twenty20 cricket, invented by the England and Wales Cricket Board in 2003, and a game in which both teams bat for a maximum of twenty overs each.

IPL – Indian Premier League, held annually in India, bringing the best players from around the world together to play in a nationally franchised T20 competition. The players are auctioned at the beginning of each season, and are generously remunerated for their time.

BUMP BALL – when the ball is hit straight into the ground by a batsman, and it flies into the hands of a fielder, leading to claims of a catch.

BUNSEN BURNER – rhyming slang for a 'turner', or a pitch that takes spin.

CHIN MUSIC – when the batsman is on the receiving end of continual bouncers and throat balls.

DIAMOND DUCK – dismissed first ball of the team's innings.

DILSCOOP – a cricket shot invented by Sri Lankan batsman Tillakaratne Dilshan, generally for use in a T20 match. On bended knee, the batsman lifts the ball off his nose and over his head, and that of the wicketkeeper.

DOLLY – an easy catch.

DOUBLE TEAPOT – a fast bowler standing with both hands on hips after a misfield, dropped catch or not-out decision with which he disagrees.

DUCK – to be dismissed without scoring a run. The term possibly derived from the shape of a 0 looking like a duck's egg.

DUCKWORTH-LEWIS – a mathematical formula for calculating a target in the case of rain delays.

GOLDEN DUCK – dismissed first ball.

GOOGLY – a ball delivered by a right arm wrist spinner that turns into, rather than away from a right-handed batsman. The ball is deceptive because it is delivered with a very similar action to a regular leg spin delivery. The Australians call it a 'Bosie' after former Australian leg-spinner and inventor of the 'googly' Bernard Bosanquet.

HAWK-EYE – a tool for broadcasters and umpires which can track the path of a ball and predict its likely path. Used for LBW decisions in international cricket.

COW CORNER – a fielder placed at deep mid-wicket, ready for a 'heave to the leg side' by an 'agricultural' style batsman.

KING PAIR – dismissed for a golden duck in both innings.

LOLLIPOP – a bad ball that is simply asking to be hit. This type of bowling is often called 'buffet bowling' by commentators such as Geoffrey Boycott, because you can just 'help yourself' to runs.

NELSON – when the score is 111. Believed to be named after Admiral Nelson, who ended up with one arm, one eye and one leg. A Double Nelson is 222, and so on. It is an unlucky number for English batsmen.

PAIR – dismissed for a duck in both innings.

PLUMB – when a bowler bowls into a batsman's pads dead in front of the wicket. The batsman should be given out LBW (Leg Before Wicket) by the umpire.

RABBIT – a tail-end batsman who is incapable of showing any sort of skill when batting i.e. easy to send back to the hutch. It can also mean a batsman, however good, who has been dismissed several times by the same bowler.

SILLY MID ON / OFF – a close fielder, positioned in front of the batsman on the on or off side of the pitch.

SLEDGING – the art of mocking a batsman to break his concentration. The Australian Test team call it 'mental disintegration'.

SLIP – a close, catching fielder behind the batsman, next to the wicketkeeper on the off side. Sometimes there are as many as four slips for a fast bowler. These fielders are said to be 'in the slips'.

SNICKO – the abbreviation for 'Snickometer', a televisual aid triggered by sound waves captured by the stump microphone. It indicates whether the ball has edged the bat.

THROAT BALL – when the ball rises sharply off a length towards the batsman's throat. This type of delivery is more commonly referred to as a 'bouncer'.

TO WALK – when a batsman admits that he is out before the umpire gives him out. Usually occurs when the wicketkeeper takes an edge, although occasionally a batsman will walk if he is caught leg-before, plumb in front of the stumps.

TRIGGERED – given out wrongly by the umpire, often very quickly after the bowler's appeal.

AN ENGLISH GAME

Pray God that no professional will ever captain England.

Lord Hawke

THE COUNTY CHAMPIONSHIP

Now far removed from amateur cricket, the professional game (or 'first-class' game) in England is dominated by the County Championship, all but one of the teams being named after English counties, the exception being Glamorgan. These county teams are called the 'Major Counties', with the 'Minor Counties' competing in their own 'Minor Counties Championship'.

Although counties played against each other as early as the eighteenth century, it wasn't until the end of the nineteenth century, in 1889, that the County Championship was formally constituted, in a meeting at Lord's Cricket Ground in London. The first matches were scheduled for the following season.

Initially the championship included only eight counties: Kent, Surrey, Sussex, Yorkshire, Lancashire, Gloucestershire, Middlesex and Nottinghamshire. However, two years later Somerset competed, and in 1895 Derbyshire, Essex, Hampshire, Leicesteshire and Warwickshire all joined. Worcestershire (1899), Northamptonshire (1905), Glamorgan (1921) and Durham (1992) have all joined since, meaning that the championship is contested by eighteen county sides under the current system. Matches are scheduled to last four days.

Should you ever reach the dizzy
heights of county cricket, always
reserve your best efforts for
Saturdays. You will then get your
name in the papers twice, on
Sunday and Monday.

J. C. Clay, Glamorgan CCC Year Book (1936)

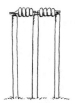

Bury me twenty-two yards from Arthur, so I can send him down a ball now and then.

Alfred Shaw, ex-England captain, who died in 1907, four years after Arthur Shrewsbury, who had committed suicide. In fact the distance between their graves measured twenty-seven yards. When someone complained to the county committee, he was told that 'Alfred always took a five-yard run-up.'

FRENCH CRICKET

The British took cricket to France as early as the eighteenth century, but it never caught on with our cousins across the Channel...

Paris, 16 April – On Monday last, a cricket match was played by some English gentlemen, in the Champs-Elysées. His Grace of Dorset was, as usual, the most distinguished for skill and activity. The French, however, cannot imitate us in such vigorous exertions of the body; so that we seldom see them enter the lists.

The Times, 2 May 1786

We got up a tolerably good match behind the Hotel Royal, on the beach at Dieppe, for the amusement of the Duchess de Berri, in the year 1829. We mustered, with some difficulty, two elevens; the bowlers pitched their balls with scientific precision; the batters defended their wickets with great skill; short and long stops were on the alert; in fact, all the performers acquitted themselves most admirably. As soon as the first innings were over, one of the party who had been most active in the display of his athletic powers, approached the Duchess's carriage in the expectation of being complimented on his exertions; instead of which, one of the suite asked the gentleman, to his utter dismay and confusion, when this game of creekay was going to begin!

The Sportsman in France, 1841

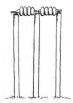

If the French noblesse had been
capable of playing cricket with
their peasants, their chateaux
would never have been burnt.

George Trevelyan

AMATEURS V PROFESSIONALS

In cricket's early years, gambling formed an important part of the game. Some matches were even contested between only two players, with huge sums waged on the winner. As the game developed into an international game in Victorian England, there was a clear split between 'amateurs' (or 'gentlemen'), generally aristocratic men who did not need to work, and played for the joy of the game, and 'professionals', who were paid to play cricket.

The professionals changed in a different dressing room, and were generally treated as second-class citizens. In 1954 Len Hutton was the first professional to captain England since Arthur Shrewsbury in 1876. More than half a century later the game is now fully professional.

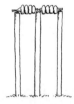

We are such sticklers for tradition
in insisting on an amateur captain,
regardless of the question of
whether he can pull his weight as
a player. The time is coming when
we will have to change our views...
when there will be no amateurs of
sufficient ability to put into
an England side.

Sir Jack Hobbs

THE OLD ENEMY

The English always come up against stern opposition in Australia, and are often less than popular. In a match between New South Wales and the Lord Harris XI in 1879, the Australian crowd started shouting 'Not out, go back!' after an umpire had ruled against an Australian batsman. One of the Lord Harris XI retaliated by shouting, 'You're nothing but the sons of convicts.' Two thousand spectators then stormed the pitch. Lord Harris himself remained steadfastly on the pitch, believing that, according to the rules, if he left the pitch he would have to concede the game. He received a number of kicks but no serious injury. After an hour and a half of rioting the game had to be abandoned.

TEATIME!

Cricket is notable as one of the only sports in which the players indulge in a scheduled break for tea during a match. A Test match is scheduled to last five days, with each day consisting of three sessions of two hours. After the first session, a forty-minute lunch is taken, and after the second session, a twenty-minute tea break is taken. The practice was introduced during the British Empire, because of the length of the game, and due to the temperatures that players were playing in. Cricket teas in the amateur game generally consist of sandwiches and cakes. Indeed, on Test match days, the BBC Test Match Special commentary team is sent cakes by listeners, so devoted are they to their tea break.

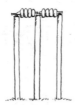

It is more than a game this cricket, it somehow holds up a mirror to English society.

Sir Neville Cordus

FAMOUS CRICKETER: SYDNEY FRANCIS BARNES

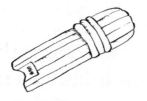

First class: 1,573 runs (12.78), 719 wickets (17.09) and 65 catches
Tests (27): 242 runs (8.06), 189 wickets (16.43) and 12 catches

There's only one captain of a side when I'm bowling – me.

Sydney Barnes

Born in April 1873 in Staffordshire, Sydney Barnes famously extracted 189 batsmen in twenty-seven Tests at an average of 16.43. His contemporaries knew him, quite simply, as the greatest bowler of all. A tall, gaunt-faced and straight-backed man with big hands and long, strong fingers, he played against very strong Australian, including players like Trumper, Hill, Armstrong, Ransford and Macartney, and South African sides of the time, making his record even more astonishing than at first glance. He could spin it, seam it or swing it in the air at a range of paces, but at a stock speed well above medium pace.

He played most of his career for his native Staffordshire, taking 1,432 wickets at a cost of eight runs apiece over twenty-two seasons. He also played cricket in the North Staffordshire, Lancashire, Central Lancashire and Bradford Leagues, taking 3,741 wickets at an average of 6.68.

He accepted £400 to tour Australia in 1901 and when he made his Test debut in a three-day match at the Sydney Cricket Ground on the 1901–2 tour, he took 5–65 and 1–74 – it was only his ninth first-class match. In the next Test he took thirteen wickets, and was unlucky to suffer a knee injury during the third Test at Adelaide, ruling him out of the remainder of the tour.

In 1902 Bill Lockwood took his place in the England side because of Barnes' perceived lack of resolve following his injury. In 1903 he was fully fit again but, following a public dispute with the Lancashire committee regarding the terms of his contract (he was seen in some quarters as lacking the right sort of temperament), he returned to League cricket, combining it with a clerical job.

When he next played for England on the 1907 tour to Australia, he took 24 wickets in the Tests at an average cost of 26 runs. He was described by Monty Noble as the best bowler in the world. Barnes then missed most of the next three years of Test cricket before returning to Australia in 1911–12 when he took 34 wickets at an average of 22 in a victorious Ashes campaign.

In the 1963 edition of *Wisden*, Barnes was selected by Neville Cardus as one of the Six Giants of the 'Wisden Century'. This was a special commemorative selection requested by *Wisden* for its 100th edition. The other five players chosen were W. G. Grace, Don Bradman, Tom Richardson, Jack Hobbs and Victor Trumper.

Like all the best bowling craftsmen, he hated batsmen and believed that every ball delivered should be their last.

Bernard Hollowood on Barnes, *Cricket on the Brain*

IT'S A FUNNY OLD GAME

Scottish cricket fan Angus Bell is the only man to
have hit a cricket ball from one continent to another.
At the end of a solo cricket tour of Eastern Europe
(which he undertook in his car), he reached Turkish
capital Istanbul where he hit a ball from one side of
the Bosphorus River to the other. Or rather, from
Europe to Asia.

Bhausahib Nimbalkar of India had scored 443 not
out with one day remaining in a first-class match. He
was only 9 runs short of the then world-record score
of 452, held by Don Bradman. But Nimbalkar was
unable to continue his innings the next day because
he had to get married.

LITERARY CRICKET

Oh, I am so glad that you have begun to take an interest in cricket. It is simply a social necessity in England.

P. G. Wodehouse, *Piccadilly Jim*

Cricket has occupied a place in the English literary imagination since its conception. It has been used to evoke English society, manners and Empire, and also as a metaphor for social change. As distinct from ordinary sports journalism, it is probably the most written-about of all our national sports. Until the twentieth century, members of the literary class were generally wealthy or aristocratic, the very same class who took to cricket worldwide during the height of Victorian expansionism. P. G. Wodehouse, J. M. Barrie, Harold Pinter, A. A. Milne and countless other writers enjoyed cricket, and it is only natural that they should have written about the game they loved, and spent so much time watching and playing.

EARLY DAYS

Last Munday youre Father was at Mr Payns and plaid at Cricket and come home pleased anuf for he struck the best Ball in the game and whished he had not anny thing else to do he wuld play Cricket all his life.

Letter from Mary Turner of East Hoathly to her son,
September 1739

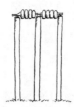

His Grace the Duke of Dorset came,
Equall'd by few, he plays with glee,
Nor peevish seeks for victory,
And for unlike the Modern way
Of blocking every ball at play,
He firmly stands with bat upright,
And strikes with athletic might,
Sends forth the ball across the mead,
And scores six notches for the deed.

John Burn, 1773

THE ALLAHAKBARRIES CRICKET CLUB

J. M. Barrie, author of *Peter Pan*, believed that cricket was 'an idea of the gods'. He was a very enthusiastic cricketer, but with very little skill; he once said of his bowling, 'I bowl so slow that if after I have delivered the ball I don't like the look of it, I can run after it and bring it back.' Undeterred by his lack of sporting prowess in 1890 he formed The Allahakbarries Cricket Club. Barrie believed 'Allah akbar' to mean 'Heaven help us', so the name was intended as a modest appraisal of the team's skill. However, it is actually an Islamic phrase meaning 'God is great'. The team included many of Barrie's literary peers, such as Arthur Conan Doyle, P. G. Wodehouse, A. A. Milne and Jerome K. Jerome. The Allahakbarries played sporadically between 1890 and 1913 with limited success. Their first match was immortalised in Barrie's *The Greenwood Hat*:

On the glorious hill-top at Albury where they were overwhelmed that day by Shere, Anon rashly allowed practice bowling, and one of the first balls sent down (by Bernard Partridge) loosened two teeth in the head of the prospective wicket-keeper, who was thus debarred from taking any further part in the game.

Watching cricket has given me more happiness than any other activity in which I have engaged. Lord's on a warm day, with a bottle, a mixed bag of sandwiches, and a couple of spare tyres in a despatch case, and I don't care who is playing whom.

A. A. Milne

An author and Allahakbarries member to have appeared in *Wisden* is Sir Arthur Conan Doyle, creator of Sherlock Holmes. His obituary was published in the 1931 edition, and although never a famous cricketer, he was more than capable, representing the Marylebone Cricket Club in first-class cricket a number of times, and on one occasion ending a match at Lord's against Cambridgeshire with bowling figures of 7 for 61.

Irish writer and poet Samuel Beckett, born in 1906, was a natural athlete, excelling at cricket as a left-handed batsman and left-arm medium-pace bowler. He represented Dublin University and played two first-class games against Northamptonshire. As a result, he became the only Nobel Laureate to have an entry in *Wisden.*

COMEDIC CRICKET

They batted through the Stone Age,
the scores became colossal,
Boycottodon was in so long
he turned into a fossil.

Poet and musician, Richard Stilgoe

Capital gain – smart sport – fine
exercise – very.

Charles Dickens, *The Pickwick Papers*

I don't think I can be expected to
take seriously a game which takes
less than three days to reach
its conclusion.

Playwright Tom Stoppard, rejecting baseball in favour
of cricket

If I knew I was going to die today,
I'd still want to hear the
cricket scores.

G. H. Hardy

PHILOSOPHERS ALL

It was a worship
in the summer sun.

Edmund Blunden

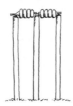

In the soft grey silence he could
hear the bump of the balls:
and from here and from there
through the quiet air the sound
of the cricket bats: pick, pack,
pock, puck: like drops of water
in a fountain falling softly in the
brimming bowl.

James Joyce, *A Portrait of the Artist as a Young Man*

As in life so in death lies a bat of renown,
Slain by a lorry (three ton);
His innings is over, his bat is laid down;
To the end a poor judge of a run.

Inscription on an English gravestone

The sand of the Desert is sodden red -
Red with the wreck of a square that broke; -
The Gatling's jammed and the Colonel's dead,
And the regiment's blind with dust and smoke.
The river of death has brimmed his banks,
And England's far, and Honour a name,
But the voice of a schoolboy rallies the ranks:
'Play up! play up! and play the game!'
Sir Henry Newbolt, from 'Vitaï Lampada'

WAUGH POEMS

One day during his Australian captaincy, Steve Waugh was training with the team fitness coach David Missen when he suggested that Missen gave the team a 'quote of the day' to inspire them onto the field. Quotes of the day soon came down to the players themselves and it was later suggested that song lyrics or even poems were recited by the players to motivate teammates, often invoking the Anzac spirit and, in the case of Waugh himself, reminding his players of the history of the game they played as a profession. Some players are reported to have written pages and pages. Shane Warne wrote a poem that, in his own words, 'wasn't quite a tear-jerker, more a motivational-type thing.'

IT'S A FUNNY OLD GAME

During a knock-up before a local cricket match at
Pentenstall, Bedfordshire, in 1955, a player hit the
cricket ball into a field, whereupon it was eaten by a
cow called Bessie. The game had to be abandoned as it
was the club's only ball.

In 1902, Australian batsman Victor Trumper broke
a window in a shoe factory 150 yards away. The
owners of the factory kept the window in its broken
state as a memorial.

The slowest delivery ever recorded took place in
New Zealand in 1921. A visiting bowler fell down a
concealed manhole as he began his run-up towards the
crease. It took rescuers fourteen hours to free the man
and after 14 hours 11 minutes the unhurt man delivered
the first ball of the over.

THE ASHES

The aim of English cricket is, in
fact, mainly to beat Australia.

Jim Laker, *Over To Me*, 1960

THE BIRTH OF THE ASHES

The term 'Ashes' was first coined after England, led by A. N. Hornby, lost to Australia for the first time on home soil at The Oval on 29 August 1882. The next day, *The Sporting Times* carried a mock obituary of English cricket, stating that: 'The body will be cremated and the ashes taken to Australia.'

At the time, cricket was at the height of its popularity, with spectators travelling the length and breadth of the country by rail to watch their favourite players. So, across a broad spectrum of society, great interest was taken in England's loss to Australia. The mock obituary therefore caught the imagination of the English public.

A few weeks later an English team consisting of eight amateurs and four professionals, captained by the Honourable Ivo Bligh, set off to tour Australia, with Bligh vowing to 'beard the kangaroo in his den and try and recover those ashes.' His Australian counterpart, Billy Murdoch, reacted by promising to defend them, using the same winning team.

Whilst Bligh's team was strong, a few of the leading English cricketers of the day were missing, most notably W. G. Grace. The itinerary of the tour had to be changed because, on the long voyage to Australia, the team's vessel, the *SS Peshawur*, collided with the *Glenroy* a few hundred kilometres south of Colombo. The players were largely fortunate to escape unhurt. Fast bowler Fred Morley was not so lucky however: he was the only player to be seriously injured, breaking a rib as a result of the collision, causing severe bruising and limiting his appearances on the tour. The injury contributed to his premature death two years later.

In the first Test, held at the Melbourne Cricket Ground, Murdoch's Australian XI were too good for Bligh's team, and won easily, by 9 wickets. The second Test, also in Melbourne, was equally one-sided, although it was England who emerged triumphant, winning by an innings amid angry debate as to which team's bowlers should be held responsible for the extreme deterioration of the pitch. Following the controversy, it was agreed to use two pitches at Sydney in the third and final match of the series – the only time two pitches have been used in the same match in Ashes history. Winning the toss, England made 247, and Australia replied with 218. In their second innings England collapsed to 123, before Dick Barlow's 7 for 40 helped to bundle the Australians out for 83. The English won the match, and with it the series.

In addition to playing three matches against the Australian national side, Bligh and his amateur colleagues took part in many social matches (the professionals in his team were not considered for selection for such games). It was at one of these social occasions, at the Rupertswood Estate outside Melbourne on Christmas Eve 1882, that Bligh was given the small terracotta urn as a symbol of the ashes he had promised to regain. It stayed on the mantelpiece at the Bligh family home until he died, forty-three years later. Florence, his wife, acting on her late husband's request, bequeathed the urn to the Marylebone Cricket Club. To this day the urn remains on show at the Lord's Museum.

THE MODERN ASHES

More than 125 years later, the Ashes is still regarded as the pinnacle of cricket for players from England and Australia, and every time they meet in a Test match, the Ashes are contested. Whereas in the nineteenth century the number of matches in each Ashes series was not standardised, today there are five matches played consecutively in each country every two years. The team which wins the most matches in a five-Test series is said to have won the Ashes. If a series is drawn, then the team that won the previous series 'retains' the Ashes.

Australia have dominated Ashes contests over the past thirty years. In Australia in 1986–87, led by Middlesex's Mike Gatting, England won the series 2–1. However, from then until 2005, Australia, benefiting from a golden generation, including all-time great players like Glenn McGrath, Shane Warne, Steve Waugh and Adam Gilchrist, held the Ashes. Michael Vaughan's side, aided by the heroic efforts of Andrew Flintoff in his greatest series, regained the urn that year, and since then England have won it two more times to Australia's one.

ASHES CRICKET GROUNDS

In Australia in 1882–83, the Melbourne Cricket Ground and the Sydney Cricket Ground were the only two Test match venues. During the 2010–11 Ashes series the same two grounds were used, but also employed were the Brisbane Cricket Ground ('The Gabba'), the Western Australia Cricket Ground in Perth ('The WACA') and the Adelaide Oval.

In England, Old Trafford, Lord's and The Oval are survivors of nineteenth-century Ashes cricket, but the authorities now spread Test matches throughout the counties as well. Grounds such as the SWALEC Stadium in Cardiff, Trent Bridge in Nottinghamshire and Edgbaston in Birmingham have all hosted Ashes Test matches.

THE BARMY ARMY

The Barmy Army is a group of English cricket fans which arranges touring parties for some of its members to follow the English cricket team on overseas tours.

Originally, 'Barmy Army' was a football chant sung by fans at many grounds, including those of Norwich City and Sheffield Wednesday. In the early 1990s, when football shirts became popular attire at cricket grounds in England, the song's repetitive line 'Barmy Army, Barmy Army, Barmy Army' found its way to domestic cricket grounds like Old Trafford and Headingley, especially during the 1993 Ashes series in England.

Throughout the 1990s, increased spending power enabled fans to take the song overseas when following the England team. The Barmy Army are not universally popular, with some commentators and spectators believing them to be a disruptive presence. The Barmy Army's unofficial leader is widely considered to be Vic Flowers, nicknamed 'Jimmy Savile' because of his resemblance to the former disc jockey.

CRICKET'S OTHER MAIN EVENTS

While the Ashes remains the pinnacle of cricket for England and Australia, there are other major events in the calendar that capture cricket lovers' imagination around the world.

CRICKET WORLD CUP – With a global audience of hundreds of millions, it is one of the biggest sporting events on the planet, especially on the Indian subcontinent where one-day cricket – consisting of one 50-over innings for each side – is more popular than Test cricket.

TWENTY20 WORLD CUP – Since 2007 the Twenty20 World Cup has battled for supremacy with the flagship competition of the 50-over game. The Twenty20 format was developed in England before it spread throughout the cricketing world. The inaugural event was held in South Africa, and won by India. The 2009 tournament was held in England and won by Pakistan, and the 2010 instalment was held in the West Indies and won by England.

TEST MATCH TROPHIES – In Test cricket, nations tend to play series against each other every few years, contesting individual trophies often named after former great players. Examples are the Frank Worrell Trophy (played between Australia and the West Indies), the Trans-Tasman Trophy (between Australia and New Zealand), the Border-Gavaskar Trophy (between Australia and India), the Wisden Trophy (between England and the West Indies) and the Warne-Muralitharan Trophy (between Australia and Sri Lanka).

INDIA

I have seen God. He bats at no. 4
for India in Tests.

Matthew Hayden on Sachin Tendulkar

The first mention of cricket in India dates from 1721, when English sailors are reported to have played a game amongst themselves in the port of Cambay. The first cricket club outside Britain was the Calcutta Cricket Club, founded in 1792 by members of the British Raj, and the first hundred scored on Indian soil was hit in 1804 by Robert Vansittart, who was playing for the Old Etonians versus a team drawn from the lesser members of the East India Company.

Indeed, cricket was initially so ingrained in British life in India that in 1946 B. V. Keskar, the General Secretary of the All India Congress Committee, stressed his view that cricket would not survive the disappearance of British rule, saying that it could only survive in an atmosphere of British culture and language. He thought it would lose its honour and grow out of date. In fact, cricket has grown beyond most commentators' expectations, and certainly beyond the expectations of Mr Keskar, since the British left India.

Ramachandra Guha writes, in *A Corner of a Foreign Field: The Indian History of a British Sport*, that while cricket was enjoyed by millions of Indians in most of India's largest cities, in Calcutta it was football, around the time of the Indian Independence movement, that was the pre-eminent sport. Had Mahatma Gandhi not forced the Indian nationalist movement away from Calcutta and towards Delhi, where cricket dominated, football may well have become the country's national sport, and not cricket.

India was granted Test match status in 1932, and their national team played their first Test match in the same year, against England at Lord's. But they had to wait for a period of 19 years,

230 days before registering their first victory in a Test match, against England in Madras in 1951.

In the 1970s players like Sunil Gavaskar, Bishen Bedi and Kapil Dev emerged as national icons, but it was not until their victory in the 1983 World Cup that the Indians began to believe that their team could be successful at the very highest level. That win acted as a catalyst and, since then, aided by huge economic growth, India has become the undisputed financial powerhouse of international cricket. It is said that the only Indians who dislike cricket are economists, who worry about its effect on absenteeism from factories and offices around the country, especially when the national team is playing a big match against bitter rivals Pakistan.

SUNIL GAVASKAR

Sunil Gavaskar, never renowned as a fast run scorer, batted through sixty overs for 36 not out in the first World Cup match at Lord's in 1975, when he thought that England's total of 334 was too great to chase.

KAPIL DEV

My effort should disprove that India cannot produce fast bowlers. For fifteen years that has been my one great motivation.

Kapil Dev, on passing Sir Richard Hadlee's record of 431 Test wickets when he dismissed Sri Lankan batsman Hashan Tillekaratne in Ahmedabad. Hadlee had taken eighty-six Tests to reach the milestone. Kapil Dev took 130

SACHIN TENDULKAR

Indian cricketers are idolised like few other sportsmen on the planet. They are superstars, making huge sums of money from the sport, and from endorsements. But there is one cricketer above all others, who, since his debut over two decades ago, has united this nation of over a billion people in the worship of cricket. Sachin Tendulkar is one of the greatest batsmen ever to play the game. Indians love him for it, and his peers respect him for it.

Chasing 279 for victory against Pakistan at Eden Gardens, Calcutta in 1999, Tendulkar clipped a ball from Shoaib Akhtar to deep square leg. Turning for the third run, he watched the ball being hurled in from the boundary. Akhtar did the same and the two collided, with Tendulkar just shy of his ground when the ball hit the stumps. He was given out, sending the one hundred thousand Indian fans into a riot. Play was suspended for an hour before Tendulkar appealed for calm. After another three-hour break for rioting, Pakistan eventually won the match, but it was remembered for all the wrong reasons.

When you bowl at him you are not just trying to get him out, you are trying to impress him. I want him to walk off thinking: 'That Flintoff, he's all right, isn't he?' I feel privileged to have played against him.

Andrew Flintoff on Sachin Tendulkar

If Sachin plays well,
India sleeps well.

Harsha Bhogle, Indian cricket commentator

Sachin Tendulkar is, in my time,
the best player without doubt –
daylight second, Brian Lara third.

Shane Warne

I want to give my six hours of
serious cricket on the ground and
then take whatever the result.

Sachin Tendulkar

INDIA FOR TOURISTS?

The subcontinent is regarded as one of the more difficult touring destinations for international cricket teams because of the combination of low pitches that take spin, the extreme heat and the intensity of the cricketing microscope.

I've done the elephant. I've done the poverty. I might as well go home.

Phil Tufnell, during the 1992–93 tour

In India you are confined to your hotel. You've just got to accept it.

Graham Gooch, during the 1992–93 tour

The players have quite reasonably talked about levels of pollution and how it has affected levels of performance... I have decided to commission an immediate report into pollution levels in Indian cities.

Ted Dexter, Chairman of the England committee
following defeat in Calcutta. The report
never materialised

THE INDIAN PREMIER LEAGUE (IPL)

When Tendulkar began playing for India, even he could not have foreseen the changes in the game that would occur during his playing career. The biggest change to the game over the past decade has been the invention of Twenty20 cricket, with players now some of the highest paid sportsmen on the planet.

The IPL is, logically, the brainchild of a party animal, for it is the most ingenious private party organised in the history of independent India.

M. J. Akbar

Far from marking the end of
nationalism, the IPL is the
ultimate triumph of that principle:
a global tournament in which the
same nation always wins.

Gideon Haigh

FAMOUS CRICKETER: SIR DONALD BRADMAN

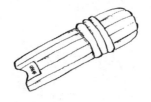

First-class: 28,067 runs (95.14), 36 wickets (37.97) and 131 catches
Tests (52): 6,996 runs (99.94), 2 wickets (36) and 32 catches

Bradman was a team in himself.
I think the Don was too good: he
spoilt the game... I do not think we
want to see another one quite like
him. I do not think we ever shall.

Jack Hobbs, 1952

Born in Cootamundra, New South Wales in 1908, Australian Sir Donald Bradman, or 'The Don', is unquestionably the greatest batsman ever to have played cricket. Statistics show that 'The Boy from Bowral' stands head and shoulders above all others in the pantheon of great Test match batsmen. A gifted tennis player, golfer and athlete, it was cricket's good fortune that Bradman turned his attention to the sport from an early age. He famously spent hours throwing a golf ball against a water tank and hitting it back with a cricket stump in his youth, honing his skills for later life.

Bradman scored his first century (115 not out) for Bowral High School against Mittagong when he was twelve years old in 1920. The following year, on a visit to the Sydney Cricket Ground, Bradman said to his father, 'I shall never be happy until I play at this ground.' In 1930, he would score a record 452 not out there.

Bradman was originally considered for selection by New South Wales as a leg-spinner. By the end of his Test career, he had bowled only twenty-six overs, taking 2 wickets for 72 runs at an average of 36.0, and an economy rate of 2.70. It turned out that he was happier with a bat in his hand.

Making his debut for Australia in 1928 against England at The Gabba in Brisbane, he was dismissed for 18 and 1 in the two innings, in a match Australia lost. For the one and only time in his Test career, he was dropped, missing the second Test, but was recalled for the third where he scored two watchful innings of 79 and 112.

Two years later, in the Ashes series of 1930, Bradman put together an astonishing set of scores to help Australia beat England. After scoring 8 in the first innings of the first Test match at Trent Bridge, he went on to record scores of 131, 254, 1, 334, 14 and 232 to post 974 runs in 7 innings, an Ashes record which still stands today.

Bradman considered the innings of 254 at Lord's his finest. Writing years later, he commented of the innings: 'Practically without exception every ball went where it was intended to go, even the one from which I was dismissed, but the latter went slightly up in the air and Percy Chapman with a miraculous piece of work held the catch.'

During the summer of 1930 England became so obsessed with stopping Bradman's run-scoring feats that in 1932 their captain devised bodyline bowling to counter his effectiveness, believing him to be susceptible to short fast bowling aimed at the ribs. To an extent the tactic was effective, as Bradman only averaged 56.57 in the series. The 'Bodyline 1932–33' chapter covers that Ashes series in greater detail.

However, by the time his final Test match came about, he needed just four runs to finish with a batting average of 100. The match was against England, at The Oval in 1948, and Bradman walked to the wicket to a standing ovation. Upon reaching the crease, the England captain, Norman Yardley, called for three cheers from his team. Bradman was out for a second-ball duck to the leg-spinner Eric Hollies and finished his career with the most famous average in cricket, 99.94. Perhaps even more staggering than this statistic, however, is the fact that during his Test career Bradman scored twenty-six per cent of the Australian team's total runs. It is unlikely that his like will be seen again on a cricket field.

IT'S A FUNNY OLD GAME

In 1977 John Snow told a High Court during the Kerry Packer hearings that he suffered nightmares about having to become an umpire when he retired as a cricketer.

In the summer of 1978, Derek Randall announced that he planned to sleep in a crash helmet for a fortnight to get used to wearing one.

In November 1982, on the England cricket tour of Australia, Derek Randall and Eddie Hemmings had to be installed in the same room after complaints from their original room-mates that they snored too much.

BODYLINE: 1932–33

If we don't beat you, we'll knock your bloody heads off.

Bill Voce, England fast bowler, to Australia's Victor
Richardson at the start of the 1932–33 series

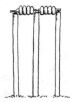

Well, we shall win the Ashes but we may lose a Dominion.

Rockley Wilson, former first-class cricketer and Douglas Jardine's coach at Winchester, on hearing that Jardine would captain MCC in Australia, 1932–33

First called 'leg theory', 'bodyline' was a tactic devised by the England cricket team, and specifically its captain Douglas Jardine, for the 1932–33 Ashes series, whereby fast bowlers would aim to take wickets by intimidating batsmen with short-pitched bowling. It was largely conceived as a way of stopping Don Bradman score runs as prolifically as he had done on the previous Ashes tour of England.

Bowlers, particularly the two fast openers, Harold Larwood and Bill Voce, were told by their captain to bowl 'leg theory' – that is, short, rising deliveries aimed at the batsman's body. The theory was that the Australian batsmen would be forced to fend the ball from under their noses, and would give catches to a packed and close leg-side field.

THE BRAINS BEHIND BODYLINE

Douglas Jardine was a Winchester- and Oxford-educated amateur cricketer of Scottish descent who played for England between 1928 and 1933. On his first tour of Australia, with the England team in 1928, he scored three consecutive hundreds in the first three tour matches, and during the second was jeered furiously by Australian supporters for scoring too slowly. Over the course of the tour, crowds took an increasing dislike to him, partly due to his success with the bat, but also because of his superior air. It is perhaps these early encounters with Australians that inspired his later bodyline tactics.

Having played very little county cricket in 1929 and 1930 due to business commitments, Jardine was never in the running for a Test place to face the Australians in 1930. The series was dominated by Don Bradman who scored 974 runs with consummate ease, helping the Australians win the Ashes 2–1. After the series was over, Jardine, on the advice of Surrey captain Percy Fender, watched video footage of Bradman facing short-pitched bowling during the series. He came to the conclusion that he had found Bradman's one weakness.

A dour, remorseless Scot, a hundred and thirty years after his time. He should have gone to Australia in charge of a convict hulk.

Jack Fingleton, the Australian opening batsman, on Jardine

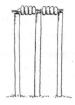

To take the most charitable view of the position, the behaviour of Australian crowds at its best, when judged by the standards accepted in the rest of the world, is not naturally good.

Douglas Jardine

Fender received letters from Australia in 1932 which described how Australian batsmen were increasingly moving across the stumps towards the off side to play the ball on the on side. He showed these letters to Jardine when it became clear that he was to captain the England side on the forthcoming tour of Australia. When Jardine was officially appointed England's captain for the 1932–33 English tour of Australia, he arranged a meeting with Nottinghamshire captain Arthur Carr, and his two fast bowlers Harold Larwood and Bill Voce, at London's Piccadilly Hotel. The subject of the meeting was Bradman, and specifically how to counter his extraordinary run-making. Jardine asked Larwood and Voce if they could bowl on leg stump and make the ball come up into the body of the batsman. The bowlers agreed they could, and that it might prove effective. Jardine also visited Frank Foster, who had toured Australia in 1911–12, to discuss field placing in Australia. It was then agreed that a cordon of close fielders on the leg side would accompany 'leg theory' bowling.

REACTIONS TO BODYLINE

Bodyline was considered by many to be intimidating and unsportsmanlike, and as such caused great controversy, especially after so many Australian batsmen sustained injuries during the series.

I don't want to see you, Mr Warner. There are two teams out there; one is trying to play cricket and the other is not.

Bill Woodfull, Australian captain, to Pelham Warner, the England manager, during the Adelaide Test match

Leave our flies alone, Jardine, they're the only flamin' friends you've got over here.

A barracker chides Jardine for swatting away a fly

The series reached crisis point at the third Test in Adelaide when Australia's captain Bill Woodfull was struck on the heart by a ball from Larwood, and wicketkeeper Bert Oldfield suffered a fractured skull from a ball by the same bowler. The crowd threatened to invade the pitch.

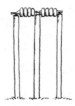

If one man jumps the fence, the whole mob will go for us.

Larwood fears for his safety after hitting Oldfield on the head

Telegrams were exchanged between the Australian and English cricketing authorities:

Bodyline bowling has assumed such proportions as to menace the best interests of the game, making protection of the body by the batsmen the main consideration. This is causing intensely bitter feeling between the players as well as injury. In our opinion it is unsportsmanlike. Unless stopped at once, it is likely to upset the friendly relationships existing between Australia and England.

Cable from the Australian Cricket Board of Control to the MCC
after the Adelaide Test, 1933

We, Marylebone Cricket Club, deplore your cable.

Part of MCC's cabled reply

England won the series, restricting Bradman to an average of 56.57. There was never a formal acknowledgement from the England authorities that bodyline bowling was unsportsmanlike, although Jardine never captained England against Australia again.

Over the two decades that followed the 1932–33 series, several cricket laws were changed to prevent the bodyline tactics employed by Douglas Jardine being repeated. The 1934 Australian tour to England featured no bodyline bowling.

It is an interesting aside that bodyline's main perpetrator, Harold Larwood, chose to retire to Australia some years later.

THE FAIRER SEX

The days of women's cricket being seen as a knicker parade must be over.

Norma Izard, manager of England's World Cup-
winning side, 1993

The history of women's cricket can be traced back to a match that reportedly took place in July 1745 between the villages of Bramley and Hambledon, near Guildford in Surrey. These early matches were not always genteel affairs: a one-day match in 1747, held at the Artillery Ground in London, spilled over into the following day after it was interrupted by crowd trouble.

Records indicate that women's matches were played regularly between villages in Sussex, Hampshire and Surrey. Other matches, often held in front of large crowds with heavy betting on the side, pitted single women against their married contemporaries.

The first women's county match was held in 1811 between Surrey and Hampshire in Middlesex, with two noblemen underwriting the game with 1,000 guineas. Originally, deliveries were bowled underarm, and while legend suggests that the round-arm bowling action was pioneered in the early nineteenth century by Christina Willes so that the ball didn't become caught in her skirt, it was in fact Tom Walker who pioneered the skill.

The first women's cricket club was formed in 1887 in Yorkshire, while in 1890 a team called the Original English Lady Cricketers toured England, playing exhibition matches to vast crowds. The team was successful on the field, although only until its manager ran off with the profits, forcing the ladies to disband. James Lillywhite's *Cricketers' Annual* for 1890 has a photograph of the team and a short article on women's cricket. 'As an exercise, cricket is probably not so severe as lawn tennis, and it is certainly not so dangerous as hunting or skating; and if, therefore, the outcome

of the present movement is to induce ladies more generally to play cricket, we shall consider that a good result has been attained.'

The Women's Cricket Association was founded in 1926, and the England team went on their first international tour to Australia in 1934–35, playing the first Women's Test match in December 1934. England won the series 2–1. It wasn't until 1979 that Lord's, the widely acknowledged home of cricket, staged its first women's Test match, between England and Australia. Originally women's Test matches lasted only three days, but since 1985 most have been played over four days.

The International Women's Cricket Council was formed in 1958 to co-ordinate women's cricket, now being played regularly in Australia, England, New Zealand, South Africa, the West Indies, Denmark and the Netherlands. Fifteen years later, in 1973, the first Women's Cricket World Cup was held in England, funded in part by businessman Jack Hayward, and won by England at Lords in front of a healthy crowd including Princess Anne.

The Women's Cricket Association handed over the running of women's cricket in England to the England and Wales Cricket Board (ECB) in 1998. In 2005, after the eighth Women's World Cup, the International Women's Cricket Council was officially integrated under the International Cricket Council, and an ICC Women's Cricket Committee was formed to consider all matters relating to women's cricket. The 2009 World Cup, the first held under the guidance of the ICC, was won by England, the first English team of either sex to win an ICC competition.

WOMEN IN THE RECORD BOOKS

Betty Wilson was the first player, male or female, to record a century and take ten wickets in the same Test match, for Australia against England at the MCG in 1958.

Women were the first sex to play an international Twenty20 match, England taking on New Zealand at Hove in 2004.

Female wicketkeepers were the first to record six dismissals in a one-day international, New Zealand's Sarah Illingworth and India's Venkatacher Kalpana both dismissing six batsmen on the same day in the 1993 World Cup.

Belinda Clark, the former Australian captain, is the only female player to have scored a double hundred in a one-day international, recording an unbeaten 229 in the 1997 World Cup against Denmark.

Pakistan's Sajjida Shah is the youngest player to appear in international cricket, playing against Ireland four months after her twelfth birthday.

Sajjida Shah also holds the record for the best bowling figures in a one-day international, taking 7 wickets for just 4 runs against Japan Women in Amsterdam in 2003.

The best match figures, 13 for 226, were recorded by Shaiza Khan for Pakistan Women against West Indies Women in Karachi in 2003–04.

RACHAEL HEYHOE-FLINT

Rachael Heyhoe-Flint epitomised women's cricket in England for more than a generation, bringing it respectability and a profile that it had not previously enjoyed. In 1963 she became the first woman to hit a six in a Test match, against Australia at The Oval. She took over the England captaincy in 1966 and remained unbeaten in six series. However, her greatest achievement was leading England to victory in the 1973 World Cup, in part because it was Heyhoe-Flint herself who was largely responsible for getting the tournament off the ground in the first place. There had never even been a men's World Cup in 1973, the first coming two years later in 1975. When she retired in 1983 she held the Test record for runs scored.

Fittingly, she was one of the first women admitted to the MCC, and in 2004 she became the first woman elected to the full committee. She also represented England at hockey.

In 2009 England batsman Claire Taylor was named one of *Wisden's* five cricketers of the year, and, as such, became the first woman to be honoured with the award in its 120-year history.

I cried all the way to the wicket. We had arrived.

Rachael Heyhoe-Flint, recalling when Lord's hosted
the 1976 women's international between
England and Australia

Women will always play for the love of the game... the enjoyment of the game must go hand in hand with skill, ability and flair.

Rachael Heyhoe-Flint and Netta Rheinberg, *Fair Play*

FAMOUS CRICKETER: KUMAR SHRI RANJITSINHJI

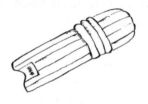

First-class: 24,692 runs (56.37), 133 wickets (34.59) and 234 catches
Tests (15): 989 runs (44.95), 1 wicket (39) and 13 catches

Cricket brings the most opposite characters and the most diverse lives together. Anything that puts very many different kinds of people on a common ground must promote sympathy and kindly feelings.

Kumar Shri Ranjitsinhji

The legendary Kumar Shri Ranjitsinhji, born in Kathiawar, India in 1872, is considered by many to be the best batsman of his era, and one of the finest of all time. Not only a prodigious run scorer, he is also feted as the inventor of the leg glance, which brought him acclaim and popularity as he became the first famous international sportsman with dark skin.

After being educated at an exclusive school in India, paid for by the Jam Sahib of Nawanagar, a distant relative, he arrived at Cambridge and began taking cricket more seriously, although, having barely played an organised game of cricket in his life, it took him four years to be selected for the university First XI, and to win a Blue. A year later, in May 1895, he made his debut for Sussex at Lord's, scoring 77 and 150 against the Marylebone Cricket Club, and went on to score 1,775 runs in the season, threatening to push W. G. Grace off the back pages of the newspapers. It was at Sussex that he formed a prolific partnership with the great C. B. Fry. Fry famously said of Ranji that he could have played three different strokes to any of the balls that he faced.

In 1896 he made his Test debut for England against Australia at Old Trafford, scoring 62 and 154 not out. He went on to break W. G. Grace's run-scoring record by posting 2,781 runs in the season, including ten centuries. George Giffen wrote of him: 'Ranji is the batting wonder of the age. His play was a revelation to us, with his marvellous cutting and extraordinary hitting to leg.'

From 1895 he scored more than 1,000 runs for ten consecutive seasons, passing 3,000 in 1899 and 1900, when he scored five double centuries. A sign of his popularity, perhaps, is that he was asked to play for seventeen different first-class teams during his career.

He led Sussex for five seasons from 1899 to 1903, but at the end of 1904 was required to return to India where his domestic responsibilities had become too great. He played only two more cricket seasons in England, in 1908 and 1912, passing 1,000 runs each time.

In 1907 Ranji's financial instability was solved when he became Maharaja Jam Sahib of Nawanagar. He was later credited for improving living conditions for people in his home state of Gujarat. During World War One he donated his country house in England, Jamnagar House at Staines, to the British government to be used as a hospital.

Later, having been appointed Chancellor of the Indian Chamber of Princes, he represented India at the League of Nations alongside his old England teammate C. B. Fry. He never married, and died in 1933 at home in Jamnagar Palace, Gujarat, India. Neville Cardus wrote of him: 'When Ranji passed out of cricket, a wonder and a glory departed from the game forever.'

POLITICAL PITCH

Politics governs everything we do –
the games we play, the way we play
them, who we play.

John Arlott

Cricket is linked to politics more closely than most other sports, partly because it was the sport played and enjoyed by the British during the spread of their Empire. The game became hugely popular in many corners of the Empire until its fall in the twentieth century, and since then, games between England and all the other Test-playing nations in particular, have taken on an added political edge, if not always for the players themselves then certainly for commentators of the game, and supporters.

Cricket has done more to consolidate the Empire than any other influence.

Lord Harris, *A Few Short Runs*, 1921

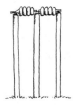

On the cricket grounds of the
Empire is fostered the spirit of
never knowing when you are
beaten, of playing for your side and
not yourself, and of never giving
up a game as lost... the future
of cricket and the Empire is so
inseparably linked.

Lord Hawke

Even politicians themselves have entered the debate about what cricket has been able to achieve in political terms. John Major, cricket fan and former British Prime Minister, is quoted as saying: 'At one level it is a game and no more; at another it helped cement an Empire and bind a Commonwealth. Its legacy is a fellowship of cricket-lovers across continents and through generations.'

Major, although not the most gifted of cricketers, did at least possess a degree of skill on the field, once scoring 50 runs in a school house match and hitting the winning runs with a straight four that whistled past the bowler's nose. He scored 33 runs in three overs to win a game on another occasion, and later got seven wickets for nine runs, including a hat-trick. Like Major, most politicians cannot claim to have been nearly as successful on the cricket field as off it. However, Alec Douglas-Home, who served as Prime Minister from October 1963 to October 1964, lays claim to being the only British Prime Minister to have played first-class cricket, representing the MCC before playing for Oxford University Cricket Club and Middlesex County Cricket Club. He played under the name 'Lord Dunglass', his title at the time. Between 1924 and 1927, Douglas-Home played ten first-class matches, scoring 147 runs at an average of 16.33 and with a best score of 37 not out. As a right-arm fast-medium bowler he took 12 wickets at an average of 30.25 with a best of 3 for 43.

A politician who seems to have possessed a warmth for the game, without ever having shown a talent for it, is Zimbabwean President Robert Mugabe who, in 1984, asserted that 'cricket civilizes people and creates good gentlemen. I want everyone to play cricket in Zimbabwe. I want ours to be a nation of gentlemen.'

But the link between cricket and politics stretches further back than to Major, Mugabe or even Douglas-Home. Modern cricketers sometimes claim that cricket and politics should not mix, but that is to ignore the very basis of the sport.

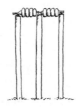

Say that cricket has nothing to do with politics and you say that cricket has nothing to do with life.

John Arlott

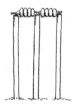

Cricket is certainly one of the
most powerful links that keep our
Empire together. It is one of the
greatest contributions which the
British people have made to the
cause of humanity.

Kumar Shri Ranjitsinhji

The British never did anything right. The one thing they did do right: they created cricket. That is the baddest [sic] game the world has ever known.

Ted Hayes, captain of the 'Homies and the Popz'
cricket team in inner-city Los Angeles, 1997

WAR AND CRICKET

No Lord's this year: no silken lawn on which
A dignified and dainty throng meanders.
The schools take guard upon a fiercer pitch
Somewhere in Flanders.
Bigger the cricket here: yet some who tried
In vain to earn a colour while at Eton
Have found a place upon an England side
Which can't be beaten.

E. W. Hornung, 'Lord's Leave', 1915

Did you see that, sir?
That means war!

MCC member at Lord's when a green baize was placed
over one of the Long Room busts, start of
the Second World War, 1939

THE WEST INDIES

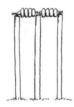

He revolted against the revolting contrast between his first-class status as a cricketer and his third-class status as a man.

C. L. R. James on the great West Indian, Learie
Constantine, in *Beyond a Boundary*, 1963

Following a campaign led by C. L. R. James, then editor of *The Nation* in Trinidad, the long period of white Test captaincy in the West Indies came to an end in 1960 when Frank Worrell became the first black cricketer to captain the West Indies cricket team for an entire series.

But not everyone agreed that native West Indians should captain their national side:

The gradual exclusion of white folk is a bad thing for West Indies cricket.

Len Hutton, former England captain

CRICKET'S FAR REACHES

I taught my kidnappers cricket. They lent me a machete and I took great pains to carve a bat – a really heavy, Gooch-type bat. The first ball took ages to carve but I had to make a whole batch because every time a boundary was hit into the jungle it was as good as lost.

Philip Halden, a British businessman kidnapped by Marxist guerrillas in Colombia, 1996

I'd say, don't give up hope. If it wasn't for the English, the Australians, the Sri Lankans and the Indians wouldn't be playing cricket. You are the masters. Maybe you are on a break right now but you will be back. You're going to fall in love with the sport again because you're going to get jealous that everyone else is falling in love with your women.

Ted Hayes, captain of the 'Homies and the Popz' cricket team in inner-city Los Angeles, 1997

THE FINAL WORD

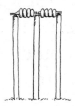

Cricket speaks in languages far beyond that of politicians.

Nelson Mandela, meeting the England team in
Soweto, 1995

HAT-TRICKS

You'll never have a better chance of getting a hat-trick.

Alec Stewart to Shane Warne as Devon Malcolm
walked out to face a hat-trick ball at the Sydney
Cricket Ground on England's 1994–95 tour.
Warne got the hat-trick

A hat-trick in cricket is achieved when a bowler takes a wicket with three consecutive balls. The origin of the term has been the subject of much debate although it is believed to have originated in cricket. The story goes that at Hyde Park in Sheffield in 1858, an All-England cricket team took on the Hallam XI. During the match, H. H. Stephenson of the All-England XI took three wickets in three balls. As was customary at the time for rewarding outstanding sporting feats, a collection was made. The proceeds were used to buy a hat, which was duly presented to Stephenson. This is reputed to be the origin of the term 'hat-trick'.

HAT-TRICK STATS

Whatever its origins, Test match hat-tricks remain hard to come by.
On average, a Test match hat-trick occurs roughly every fifty Tests.
At least one bowler from each of the ten nations that play Test cricket
has taken a Test hat-trick and, at the time of writing, India is the
only country against whom nobody has taken a hat-trick.

Australian bowler Fred Spofforth dismissed three English
batsmen (Vernon Royle, Francis MacKinnon and Tom Emmett)
with consecutive deliveries at the Melbourne Cricket Ground on 2
January 1879 to take the first hat-trick in Test cricket, in only the
third Test match in history.

Hugh Trumble of Australia became the first player to take two
hat-tricks in Test cricket and the only player ever to have taken
two Ashes hat-tricks, when at the MCG in 1904 he dismissed three
English batsmen in the second innings, having not even bowled in
the first innings. That Test match turned out to be Trumble's final
match in first-class cricket.

At his benefit match against Somerset at Lord's in 1907, Albert
Trott took two hat-tricks in the same innings, thus severely
shortening the game and depriving himself of much gate money.
'I'm bowling myself into the workhouse,' he moaned. In fact,
Trott's first hat-trick was followed by another wicket, meaning he
took four wickets in four balls, with the fifth ball missing the off-
stump by inches.

A player has taken two hat-tricks in the same Test match only once. Playing for Australia against South Africa in the first match of the 1912 Triangular Tournament at Old Trafford, leg-spinner Jimmy Matthews took a hat-trick in South Africa's first and second innings.

Pakistani fast bowler Wasim Akram is the third cricketer to have taken a Test hat-trick more than once. Akram took his two Test match hat-tricks just over a week apart, in consecutive matches against Sri Lanka in 1999.

Three players have taken a hat-trick on their Test debut: English medium-pace bowler Maurice Allom in 1930, New Zealand off-spinner Peter Petherick in 1976, and Australian pace bowler Damien Fleming in 1994.

Jimmy Matthews, Englishman Dominic Cork, Pakistani Mohammad Sami and West Indian Jermaine Lawson have all achieved hat-tricks without fielding assistance.

No player has taken four wickets in four balls in a Test match, although this feat has been accomplished in one-day cricket, by Sri Lankan Lasith Malinga in 2007 against South Africa.

The oldest player to take a hat-trick in Test cricket is English off-spinner Tom Goddard, against South Africa during the 1938–39 series – he was aged 38 years 87 days.

Indian Irfan Pathan is the only bowler to have taken a hat-trick in the first over of a Test match.

West Indian Courtney Walsh and Australian Merv Hughes are the only two players from opposing teams to have taken hat-tricks in the same series.

All Test hat-tricks by Pakistani bowlers – Wasim Akram, Abdul Razzaq and Mohammad Sami – have been against Sri Lanka.

It's amazing how many hat-trick balls are not bowled in the right place. For Hooper I knew that I had to pitch it right up, almost half-volley length. I have watched the replay a thousand times to check if there was any way that it couldn't have been given, but there definitely wasn't.

Dominic Cork following his hat-trick against West Indies at Old Trafford in 1995. His victims were Richie Richardson, Junior Murray and Carl Hooper

Three bowlers (Pakistani Wasim Akram and Englishmen Maurice Allom and Chris Old) have each taken four wickets in five balls, just missing out on hat-tricks in the process.

Peter Siddle is the only bowler to have taken a Test match hat-trick on his birthday. When he claimed the hat-trick, during the first Test in Brisbane in 2010, Australia equalled England as the team with the most Test match hat-tricks. Each has eleven.

CRICKET COMMENTATORS

This bowler's like my dog: three short legs and balls that swing each way.

Brian Johnston

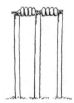

The bowler's Holding, the batsman's Willey.

Brian Johnston, when West Indian fast bowler
Michael Holding was bowling to England's Peter
Willey in a Test match at The Oval in 1976

Because a game of cricket lasts so long, its followers place great importance on the quality of its commentators. Characters abound in cricket commentary, but here are four of its greatest exponents:

JOHN ARLOTT – born in February 1914, John Arlott was an English commentator for BBC *Test Match Special*, as well as a journalist, poet, wine connoisseur and author.

After being invited to make a public radio address to George VI on VE Day, 1945, he attracted the attention of the BBC, and subsequently joined the BBC as the Overseas Literary Producer in 1946.

In 1946 he was asked to cover a couple of India's warm-up games on their tour of England. He was so popular that he was invited to continue to commentate on further matches, including the Test matches that summer, thereby initiating a thirty-four-year career as a cricket commentator for the BBC. He experienced some resentment from his colleagues in the commentary box at first, clashing notably with E. W. Swanton, but he rapidly found his niche, and from 1946 to 1980 he covered every single home Test match. He only went on two overseas England tours, to South Africa in 1948–49 and Australia in 1954–55.

BRIAN JOHNSTON – born in Hertfordshire in 1912, 'Johnners' was a cricket commentator and presenter from 1946 until his death in 1994. Educated at Eton and New College, Oxford, Johnston obtained a third-class degree in History in 1934 before joining his family's coffee business, where he worked until the outbreak of war.

Having served in the war and been awarded the Military Cross in 1945, he then joined the BBC in 1946 at what was the beginning of a forty-eight-year media career. He began his cricket commentary career in television, becoming the BBC's first cricket correspondent in 1963, but was later moved to radio because it was thought his comedic talents were wasted on television. There he became a national institution on *Test Match Special*, often bursting into fits of laughter while trying to continue to commentate. Upon his death, *The Daily Telegraph* described Johnston as 'the greatest natural broadcaster of them all'.

RICHIE BENAUD – born in October 1930 in New South Wales, Benaud is a former Australian leg-spinner and captain who, since his retirement from international cricket in 1964, has become a highly regarded television commentator. He had already been awarded an OBE in 1961 for services to cricket.

Cricket journalist Gideon Haigh described him as 'perhaps the most influential cricketer and cricket personality since World War Two.' In his review of Benaud's autobiography *Anything But*, Sri Lankan cricket writer Harold de Andrado wrote: 'Richie Benaud, possibly next to Sir Don Bradman, has been one of the greatest cricketing personalities as player, researcher, writer, critic, author, organiser, adviser and student of the game.'

In 2004, Benaud starred in a series of television advertisements for the Australian Tourism Commission, aimed at promoting Australia as a tourist destination. The advert featured him in various scenic locations uttering his signature comment, 'Marvellous!'

JONATHAN AGNEW – born in Macclesfield, England in April 1960, 'Aggers', as he is affectionately known, is a former Leicestershire and England fast bowler who turned to radio upon retirement and became a regular on BBC *Test Match Special*. Agnew was commentating with Brian Johnston for an England v West Indies Test match in August 1991 when they produced a piece of commentary which has been voted by BBC listeners as the 'greatest piece of sporting commentary ever'. In a review of the day's play, Johnston was describing how Ian Botham, while batting, had overbalanced and tried to step over his stumps. Botham was given out 'hit wicket' and Agnew's comment on the debacle was: 'He just couldn't quite get his leg over.' The innuendo provoked a lengthy period of laughter and giggling, most notably by Johnston, who tried to continue commentating through his giggles.

Famous Cricketer: Sir Garfield St Aubrun Sobers

First-class: 28,315 runs (54.87), 1,043 wickets (27.74) and 407 catches

Tests (93): 8,032 runs (57.78), 235 wickets (34.03) and 109 catches

Nobody in cricket has given
me more sheer delight than
Sobers. His brilliance has been
breathtaking.

Jack Fingleton, *Fingleton on Cricket* (1972)

West Indian Garfield St Aubrun Sobers is widely acknowledged as the most talented all-round cricketer ever to have played the game. Versatility in a cricketer sometimes means that quality in one or other skill is sacrificed, but not in Sobers' case. He can lay claim to having been one of the most stylish batsmen of all time, one of the best fielders, and certainly one of the most effective bowlers of his generation, being three bowlers in one. While it was often his batting that stole the limelight, he often took the new ball for club and country, bowling left-arm fast, either swinging the ball back into right-handers with ease or letting the angle send the ball across the batsman. He could also bowl 'chinamen' and googlies, although more often he bowled left-arm orthodox spin and this was the skill with which he originally earned his place in the West Indies side.

Sobers was born in Bridgetown, Barbados in 1936. His father, a sailor, was killed during World War Two, and although Sobers grew up in relative poverty, he spent his days kicking a football, playing golf and basketball, and of course cricket. He first represented Barbados at cricket aged sixteen against the touring Indians in 1953, playing as a specialist left-arm finger spinner. He took seven wickets in the match, bowling accurately and with guile.

In 1954 he made his Test debut, taking four wickets and batting at number 9. Only four years later he was to break Len Hutton's world Test record by scoring 365 not out against Pakistan in Jamaica. He scored 824 runs in the series at an average of 137. He was still only twenty-one years old.

He played every Test match for West Indies between 1955 and 1972, humbling bowling attacks all over the world, from English sides with Brian Statham and Fred Trueman to Australian attacks including Alan Davidson and Richie Benaud. In 1972, captaining the Rest of the World XI against Australia, spearheaded by Dennis Lillee in his pomp, Sobers played arguably his finest innings, hitting 254 in the second innings. Donald Bradman, who was watching, described the innings as 'probably the best ever seen in Australia, one of the historic events of cricket'.

With increasing demands on the modern player, it is unlikely the world will again see such an all-round cricketer as Sobers. Everything about Sobers was individual and unique: his high backlift and extravagant follow-through, and even the way he walked to the crease with long, relaxed strides giving at the knee. When the Queen visited Barbados in 1975 she took the opportunity to honour Sobers with a knighthood on his own territory. In retirement his main hobbies are golf and racing.

BAD BOYS AND TROUBLEMAKERS

Ian Botham represents everything that's the best in Britain. He's Biggles, the VC, El Alamein, the tank commander, he's everything. I mean, how could a schoolboy not want to be like Ian Botham?

Tim Hudson, Ian Botham's agent, 1985

Like any sport, cricket attracts its bad boys. Over the years there have been loveable rogues like Ian Botham and W. G. Grace, but there have also been those who have, through their ill-judged actions, brought the supposedly noble game of cricket into disrepute, such as the instigator of 'bodyline', Douglas Jardine, or shamed South African captain Hansie Cronje (see 'Match- and Spot-Fixing' below).

Even as far back as the late nineteenth century cricket attracted bad boys. In 1897, the captain of Yorkshire Cricket Club, Lord Hawke, imposed a ban on left-arm spinner Bobby Peel as a punishment for his drunkenness. Peel had come on to the pitch and urinated in front of the captain.

IAN BOTHAM

Part of what the cricket-watching public liked about Ian Botham was that he seemed real, raw and cavalier in his approach to his profession. He certainly fell into the 'loveable rogue' category. While Bob Willis was giving an interview during the England tour of Australia in 1982–83, Ian Botham was lobbing banana skins at him from a dressing-room window. Without turning his head Willis said, 'He lives on them, you know.'

And it wasn't only his teammates he riled. In September 1982, Botham was thrown into a swimming pool at the Cadbury Country Club, Weston-super-Mare, by a thirty-year-old motor mechanic,

Mr Bent. Bent later told friends that he thought Botham was behaving badly. Four years later Botham became the first cricketer to be punished for drug use and was suspended for two months for 'bringing the game into disrepute by using cannabis'.

Botham certainly had an effect on those playing around him. When England looked like losing the third Cornhill Test match in 1981, two members of the Australian team, Dennis Lillee and Rodney Marsh, backed England to win at 500–1. When England won after a hundred by Botham and eight wickets from Bob Willis, and news of their bet leaked, there was a public outcry. Botham's charm certainly worked on at least two people though. Mike Brearley, often his England captain, is quoted as saying of Botham: 'I don't know what it is, but I take stuff from him I'd clip other guys in the ear for.'

And of course, Botham's mother didn't see the rebel in her son: 'He's a big softy really – full of life and fun, very determined on the cricket pitch but gentle as they come. He was the only teenage boy I knew who would always stop and talk to babies and children in the street.'

A FEW OTHER NAUGHTY BOYS

DAVID BOON – The Australian batsman wrote his name into cricketing folklore when he drank fifty-two cans of beer on the flight to London ahead of the 1989 Ashes series. It was suggested in some quarters that the Tasmanian speed limit be lowered to 52 kph as a tribute.

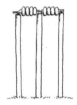

ANDREW 'FREDDIE' FLINTOFF – Burly Lancashire all-rounder Flintoff, hero of the 2005 Ashes triumph over Australia, was blasted by the press when he was seen on a pedalo off the coast of St Lucia at 3 a.m. after an England World Cup match. He capsized the pedalo in an incident that became known as 'Fredalo', and was stripped of the vice-captaincy. Flintoff commented: 'It is no secret that I enjoy going out for a drink every now and then.'

DENNIS LILLEE – During the Perth Test in 1979, Lillee came to the wicket holding an aluminium cricket bat. When Mike Brearley objected, the umpire asked Lillee to change bats. He refused and walked off. A few minutes later he reappeared, still holding the aluminium bat. At this point Greg Chappell intervened, persuading Lillee, eventually, to go back to using a traditional wooden cricket bat. In February 1980, despite the fact that Lillee and a backer had spent £400,000 developing aluminium bats, Lord's revised Law 6 to stipulate that 'the blade of the bat shall be made of wood.'

IAN CHAPPELL – During the World Series Cricket 'Supertest' in 1979, the Sydney crowd booed when Ian Chappell dropped two catches. On catching a third successfully, Chappell turned and gave a double V-sign to the crowd.

THROWING

DEFINITION: Throwing, commonly referred to as 'chucking', is an illegal bowling action which occurs when a bowler moves their arm from a bended position, and straightens it during delivery of the ball. The Laws of Cricket specify that a bowler's arm must be fully extended and rotated around the shoulder to impart velocity to the ball. Throws are not allowed. If the umpire believes that the ball has been thrown, he will call a 'no-ball', which means the batsman cannot be given out from that delivery.

The issue of throwing is often highly emotive, with accusers considering that bowlers delivering the ball with an illegal action are in fact cheating.

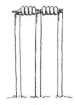

Throwing is unfair. It is insidious, infectious and a menace to the game. It must be stopped and the exchange of cables between countries will not do it. Unless it is stopped before the Australians arrive, a serious position is imminent.

Tom Smith, Association of Cricket Umpires, in *The Cricketer*, 1960

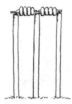

It's like standing in the middle of a darts match.

Jim Laker, commenting on the legality of the bowling
actions of Ian Meckiff and Jimmy Burke during the
1958–59 MCC tour of Australia

Since the birth of the overarm delivery, a number of players have been called for throwing in international matches, invariably creating controversy and occasionally destroying careers. Often, however, players are able to modify their bowling actions to satisfy critics and umpires.

Eleven players have been called for throwing in a Test match, dating back to Australian bowler Ernie Jones, who was no-balled at Melbourne in 1898. Since then the bowlers called for throwing in a Test match are Tony Lock, Geoffrey Griffin, Haseeb Ahsan, Ian Meckiff, Abid Ali, Syed Kirmani, David Gower, Henry Olonga, Muttiah Muralitharan and Grant Flower.

One of the most famous recent cases of a player being called for throwing is that of Muttiah Muralitharan. During the second Test between Sri Lanka and Australia at the Melbourne Cricket Ground on Boxing Day 1995, Australian umpire Darrell Hair called the Sri Lankan spinner for 'throwing' in front of a crowd of 55,000. Muralitharan was no-balled seven times in the space of three overs, each time by Hair, who believed that the bowler was bending his arm and straightening it during the delivery. The controversy continued during Australia's two-day-long innings. Muralitharan bowled a further thirty-two overs from umpire Steve Dunne's end without protest from either Dunne or Hair. Muralitharan's action was cleared by the ICC in 1996 when they decided his action created an optical illusion of 'throwing', but he continued to divide opinion until, in 2011, he retired from Test cricket as the highest wicket-taker in history.

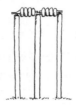

Cricket has permitted the public humiliation of a player... it is not a performance I'd care to witness again.

Peter Roebuck commenting on Darrell Hair's calling of Muttiah Muralitharan

MATCH- AND SPOT-FIXING

The fixing of part or all of cricket matches is perhaps one of the greatest challenges faced by cricketing authorities today. There are two main types of fixing in cricket. 'Match-fixing' occurs when a match is played to a pre-determined result. 'Spot-fixing' refers to a specific part of the game being fixed.

The ultimate cricketing bad boy was, perhaps, born-again Christian and South African captain Hansie Cronje, who in the late 1990s was regarded as representing all that was good about the game of cricket. That was before he was caught taking thousands of pounds from Indian bookmakers to influence and fix games at the turn of the century. He disgraced South African cricket and was banned from playing or coaching cricket for life. Two years later he died in a plane crash, aged only thirty-two.

In 2010, three Pakistan cricketers were sanctioned by the International Cricket Council for bowling no-balls to order during a Test match against England at Lord's. Captain Salman Butt and fast bowlers Mohammad Asif and Mohammad Amir were banned for varying lengths of time. Embarrassingly for all concerned, Amir was named Pakistan's Man of the Series on the day that the story broke in the British newspapers. Amir had, for a brief time, become one of cricket's brightest prospects.

Still, some profess Amir's innocence:

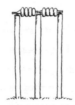

No, I don't believe it. It is propaganda. Mohammad Amir is the hero of Gujjar Khan.

A fruit salesman in Mohammad Amir's home town of
Gujjar Khan, 35 miles south-east of Islamabad

IT'S A FUNNY OLD GAME

In 1930, Columbia Records contracted Don Bradman to make a record. They thought that he would be giving a talk on cricket, and were somewhat surprised when the recording he made was of his piano renditions of the popular dance numbers 'An Old Fashioned Locket' and 'Our Bungalow of Dreams.'

Playing for Somerset against Nottinghamshire in 1930, C. C. Case was so surprised to be given out 'hit wicket' that in his trance he left the pitch carrying one of the stumps, thinking it was his bat.

Jim Laker's first wicket in first-class cricket occurred when he was bowling against R. N. Exton at Kingston in 1946. The fielder was pulling a sweater over his head when the ball came his way. He caught it by closing his legs on it.

GREAT WORLD CUP INNINGS

There is probably a greater premium on temperament for a batsman than for any player in any branch of sport.

Sir Donald Bradman, *The Art of Cricket*, 1958

Sir Donald Bradman, writing in 1958, could not have foreseen the advent of one-day international cricket and the World Cup, but he still knew what made a great batsman. The World Cup is now cricket's showpiece, a competition held every four years in the glare of the media and hundreds of millions of fans worldwide. As a batsman, it is the best time to deliver, and all of the batsmen in this chapter were able to stay calm to play extraordinary innings in pressurised situations. So, here are some of the finest innings in World Cup history, from the inaugural competition, held in England in 1975, to the 2011 competition in India.

CLIVE LLOYD: 102
WEST INDIES V AUSTRALIA – FINAL, LORD'S, 21 JUNE 1975

Lloyd led West Indies to their first World Cup win with what is acknowledged by some as the greatest World Cup innings of them all. The West Indian captain was dropped on 26 but made the most of the let-off by blasting a hundred, cutting and driving with huge power, off 82 balls. Not content with his batting heroics, he then bowled a tidy twelve-over spell of 1 for 38 as West Indies defeated Australia by 17 runs.

VIVIAN RICHARDS: 138 NOT OUT
WEST INDIES V ENGLAND – FINAL, LORD'S,
23 JUNE 1979

The West Indies were reeling at 99 for 4 when Viv Richards, the only man to have played both World Cup football and World Cup cricket, took the game by the scruff of the neck, changing the course of the match with a magnificent 138 not out, in partnership with Collis King who himself scored 86 from 66 balls. He finished the innings off in style, smashing the last ball for six.

KAPIL DEV: 175 NOT OUT
INDIA V ZIMBABWE – GROUP STAGE,
TUNBRIDGE WELLS, 18 JUNE 1983

Kapil Dev announced India's entrance onto the ODI stage with an impeccable 175 off just 138 balls against Zimbabwe. In the two previous tournaments India had won just one game, against East Africa. They had even lost to Sri Lanka, who were a long way off gaining Test match status as a cricket-playing nation. Kapil railed the Indian side against World Cup debutants Zimbabwe after coming to the crease with his team at 9 for 4. India eventually made 266 off their allotted sixty overs, with the next highest scorer making just 24. More importantly, however, Kapil Dev's innings injected his side with confidence and they eventually won the tournament, sending a billion Indian cricket fans into wild celebrations.

ARAVINDA DE SILVA: 107
SRI LANKA V AUSTRALIA – FINAL, LAHORE,
17 MARCH 1996

Sri Lanka were 23–2, chasing 242 to win, when de Silva came to the crease. He proceeded to play the innings of his life to lead Sri Lanka to a first World Cup triumph. He finished with 107 from 124, and ensured his team won the tournament with three overs to spare. His innings gains special significance because he produced this, his most memorable innings, in a World Cup Final against the world's best bowling attack, including Glenn McGrath and Shane Warne.

STEVE WAUGH: 120 NOT OUT
AUSTRALIA V SOUTH AFRICA – SUPER SIXES
STAGE, HEADINGLEY, 13 JUNE 1999

Australia were facing elimination from the competition until Waugh turned things around with an innings of character and determination. Herschelle Gibbs lent him a hand when, with Waugh on 56, he dropped a catch by celebrating prematurely. Folklore says that Waugh told Gibbs he had 'just dropped the World Cup', and whether this is true or not, he had. Gibbs' hundred earlier in the match was forgotten as Waugh went on to hit 120 not out and keep Australia's hopes in the competition alive. They went on to beat South Africa again in the semi-final.

RICKY PONTING: 140 NOT OUT
AUSTRALIA V INDIA – FINAL,
JOHANNESBURG, 23 MARCH 2003

Ponting took 74 balls to reach his half-century, but then plundered 90 off his next 47 balls, including eight sixes, with Harbhajan Singh, Javagal Srinath and Zaheer Khan coming in for particularly harsh treatment. He left India chasing a daunting 359 for victory and they never got close, finishing 125 runs short.

ADAM GILCHRIST: 149
AUSTRALIA V SRI LANKA – FINAL,
BARBADOS, 28 APRIL 2007

The farcical conclusion to the 2007 World Cup, when Sri Lanka batted in near darkness after the intervention of the Duckworth-Lewis method, meant that Adam Gilchrist's innings in the final does not receive the recognition it perhaps deserves. Gilchrist hit the highest score in a final, smashing eight sixes and thirteen fours off 104 balls. It was the man who redefined the notion of the wicketkeeper-batsman who had defeated Sri Lanka, rather than the Duckworth-Lewis method.

KEVIN O'BRIEN: 113
IRELAND V ENGLAND – GROUP STAGE,
BANGALORE, 2 MARCH 2011

England set Ireland 328 to win in a group match in Bangalore in the 2011 tournament. With his team struggling at 111–5, O'Brien, a twenty-six-year-old marketing and advertising graduate, could have been forgiven for thinking Ireland were on the road to defeat. But the man who plays his cricket for Railway Union Cricket Club in Ireland, smacked the fastest century in World Cup history, reaching his hundred off 50 balls and going on to hit 113, as he guided his side to the biggest World Cup upset of all time.

Ger O'Brien, his brother and President of Kevin's club in Ireland, put it best when he said, 'It is such a great day for Irish cricket. Some bookmakers had Ireland at 400–1 at one stage. I wish I'd not kept my money in my pocket.'

M. S. DHONI: 91 NOT OUT
INDIA V SRI LANKA – WORLD CUP FINAL,
MUMBAI, 2 APRIL 2011

Sehwag and Tendulkar were back in the pavilion, and Yuvraj Singh, India's star performer throughout the tournament, was due in at number 5. But India's captain M. S. Dhoni, sensing the need for a right-hander at the crease to combat Sri Lanka's off-spinners, and perhaps driven by a sense of captain's responsibility, promoted himself above Yuvraj. On the back of a terrible run of form, he played the innings of his life, batting alongside Gautam Gambhir who himself made 97, and saw India to World Cup glory with an unbeaten 91, including a huge 6 to send a billion Indian cricket fans into euphoria. Michael Atherton, writing in *The Times*, thought that 'the greatest innings ever played by a captain in a World Cup final was Clive Lloyd's monumental hundred against Australia at Lord's in the inaugural tournament in 1975, and if this was not its equal then it was not far behind'.

IT'S A FUNNY OLD GAME

New Zealand have the dubious honour of scoring the lowest Test innings, against England at Eden Gardens, Auckland in 1955. Only one man reached double figures and five batsmen scored ducks, England winning the match by an innings and 20 runs.

On 18 June 1893 the first game of cricket in Romania was played, between XIs representing Bucharest and Braila. The Crown Prince and Princess were present.

Sourav Ganguly is the only cricketer to have won four successive 'Man of the Match' awards in one-day internationals.

FAMOUS CRICKETER: DENNIS LILLEE

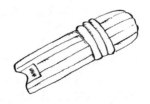

First-class: 2,377 runs (13.90), 882 wickets (23.46) and 67 catches
Tests (70): 905 runs (13.71), 355 wickets (23.92) and 23 catches
One-day Internationals (63): 240 runs (9.23), 103 wickets (20.82)
and 10 catches

Few fast bowlers have had a finer physique or technique, or such a gloriously flowing action.

John Arlott, *An Eye for Cricket*

Dennis Keith Lillee (1949–) made his first-class debut for Western Australia in 1969 at the tender age of twenty, and with his fierce skills as a fast bowler took 32 wickets in the season. The following year he represented his state against the touring English side, and was selected for his debut Test in Adelaide a few weeks later. When Australia took on a Rest of the World XI in a four-match series the following season, Lillee announced himself as the complete fast bowler with 23 wickets, including 8 for 29 in Perth, when he bowled out the World XI (including Garry Sobers at number 7) for 59.

In the 1972 Ashes series against England he was exceptional, taking 31 wickets, having learned a leg-cutter from John Snow, and also having shortened his run-up on the advice of countryman Ray Lindwall. It was in 1974–75 that he formed a legendary partnership with Jeff Thomson, the other incredibly fast Australian bowler of the time. During the Ashes series that year, banners could be found at Australian grounds, adorned with the somewhat poetic: 'Ashes to Ashes, dust to dust: if Lillee don't get you, Thommo must!' Thomson took 33 wickets in the series, and Lillee 25, as England were simply blown away. The pair were to terrorise Test teams around the world over the next few years, forming one of the great bowling partnerships of all time.

In the late 1970s Lillee was not seen in Test cricket for a couple of years. He was attracted to Kerry Packer's financially lucrative breakaway World Series Cricket in May 1977 and became one of its brightest lights, taking 79 wickets at an average of 23, and out-bowling West Indian fast bowlers Andy Roberts and Michael Holding. When he returned he had lost some of his youthful pace and aggression, but by sheer determination remained the best fast bowler in the world until he retired, taking 85 wickets at an average of 21 runs in Tests in 1981.

He was a national hero in Australia, adored by cricket fans for his attacking style of bowling. He did, however, sometimes let himself down, like when he asked the Queen for her autograph when the teams were introduced to her during the Centenary Test in Melbourne, or when he used an aluminium bat as a marketing ploy in Perth. However, he was one of the game's brightest stars and since his retirement has done much good work as a bowling coach, especially in India where he has been responsible for the production of a number of excellent fast bowlers.

CRICKET'S WIT

I took an American friend to watch
her first game of cricket. She took
one look at the umpires and said,
'What are the butchers for?'

Alan Henderson

In 1863, a strange game of cricket took place. A team of one-legged men took on a team of one-armed men. The one-legged team won by 21 runs, their best player being a man with no legs, named Letford, who batted at number 10 and scored ten in the first innings. The *Manchester Daily Examiner* is reported to have assessed his value to the team with the quote, 'Without him, the eleven would not have had a leg to stand on.'

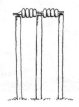

Keep corpse on ice till innings declared.

Telegram sent by coroner Dr E. M. Grace (W. G.'s brother) from the Oval to his office in Bristol when they asked him to preside over an inquest

When Fred Trueman was asked to suggest a title for his autobiography, he replied: 'The Definitive Volume of the Finest Bloody Fast Bowler that Ever Drew Breath.'

Dining at the University Arms in Cambridge, Fred Trueman spent a long time studying the French menu. Eventually, he pointed to the bottom of the menu and said to the waiter, 'Aye, and I'll have that for sweet.' He had chosen *'Jeudi, le douzième de mai.'*

My definition of a foreigner
is someone who doesn't
understand cricket.

Anthony Couch

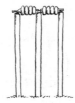

Facing a fast bowler is
like standing in the outside lane
of the M1, and when a car is
twenty-two yards away, try to
get out of the way.

Alec Stewart

The last positive thing England did for cricket was invent it.

Ian Chappell

I just want to get into the middle and get the right sort of runs.

England batsman Robin Smith, on suffering from diarrhoea on a cricket tour of India

Pitches are like wives – you can never tell how they're going to turn out.

Len Hutton

As journalist Dudley Doust was travelling in Ian Botham's car through Somerset, he tuned into Radio 3. Botham turned it off, saying, 'None of that Radio 3 stuff. I'm Ian Botham, not Mike Brearley.'

During a county championship match between Glamorgan and Somerset, Glamorgan pace bowler Greg Thomas beat Vivian Richards' bat a couple of times before provoking the legendary West Indian batsman by saying 'It's red, round and weighs about five ounces, in case you were wondering.' The very next ball, Richards hit a huge six out of the ground, into a river and said to Thomas, 'Greg, you know what it looks like. Now go and find it.'

I don't ask Kathy to face Michael
Holding. So I don't see why I
should be changing nappies.

Ian Botham explains his approach to fatherhood

No good hitting me there, mate:
nothing to damage.

Derek Randall to Dennis Lillee, pointing to his skull
after being hit there

What's the point in 'O' Levels?
They don't help you play cricket.

Ian Botham

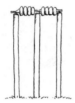

Tufnell! Can I borrow your brain?
I'm building an idiot.

One of the funnier Australian barrackers as Phil
Tufnell was pilloried by the crowd in Newcastle,
Ashes series, 1994–95

Australian captain Alan Border nicknamed Merv Hughes 'Fruitfly', because he was Australia's biggest pest.

How anyone can spin a ball the width of Gatting boggles the mind.

Martin Johnson, in *The Independent*, on Shane Warne's 'Ball of the Century', which bowled Mike Gatting in 1993

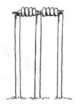

If it had been a cheese roll, it would never have got past him.

Graham Gooch pokes fun at Mike Gatting, referring
to Shane Warne's 'Ball of the Century'

With the possible exception of Rolf Harris, no other Australian has inflicted more pain and grief on Englishmen since Don Bradman.

Mike Walters in the *Daily Mirror*, reflecting on Steve Waugh's retirement

Ponting resembles George W. Bush, and leads like him too.

Tim de Lisle in *The Times*

He fell in love with himself at a very young age and has remained faithful ever since.

Dennis Lillee on Geoffrey Boycott

Use Botham to Roll the Pitch!

Message on a New Zealand banner in February 1983, a reference to Botham's perceived weight problem at the time

ENGLISH HONESTY

One is always a little nervous when watching England bat.

Peter May, England chairman of selectors, 1981

For much of the 1980s and 1990s the English cricket team were, if not a laughing stock, then certainly seen by most of their opponents as easy prey on the cricket field. They were habitually beaten by Australia in the Ashes, and by the West Indies too, with their legendary pace attack. But a peculiar component of Englishness is the ability to laugh at one's own fate. During the decline of the 1980s and 90s, former and current players, journalists and commentators from England all joined in what the Australians like to call a little bit of 'pommie bashing'. No one can say they weren't being honest!

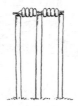

England have only three major problems. They can't bat, they can't bowl and they can't field.

Martin Johnson, *The Independent*, 1986

If we had shown the kind of attitude and guts during the war that our cricketers have in the West Indies, Hitler would have walked all over us.

Brian Close, former England captain, 1986

I can remember some good Saturdays against the West Indies before – the only trouble is that the Thursdays, Fridays, Mondays and Tuesdays were a bit of a disaster.

John Emburey, after his first day as England captain against West Indies, 1988

England's seventeenth choice.

Alan Igglesden, as described by his England team
manager Micky Stewart upon his selection at the
Oval in 1989

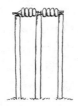

He crossed the line between eccentricity and idiocy far too often for someone who was supposed to be running English cricket.

Ian Botham on Ted Dexter

Despite a surprise Ashes victory in Australia in 1986–87, England went on to win only one other Test series in the 1980s, against newcomers to Test cricket, Sri Lanka. The decline continued through the 1990s, a situation not helped by petty disagreements between players and selectors. Their poor performances were sometimes blamed on the demands placed on players by their county cricket teams. England could rarely field a full-strength team on their tours because of injuries.

There was a string of disappointing results in the mid 1990s as England did not win a Test match for two and half years. A surprise win against South Africa in 1998 was England's first five-Test series win since 1986–87, but this would be a false dawn as they lost a home Test series against New Zealand 2–1 shortly after.

England, the premier side in the world at the beginning of the twentieth century, were ranked as the worst Test nation at the end of it.

A fart competing with thunder.

England captain Graham Gooch on his side's Ashes
tour, 1990–91

We were the better side for three days. Then we got blown away inside an hour.

Michael Atherton, considering defeat in Trinidad, 1993–94

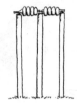

I don't think he could motivate a stuffed mullet at the moment.

Allan Lamb after England's 3–1 Ashes defeat under
manager Keith Fletcher, 1995

FAMOUS CRICKETER: ANDREW FLINTOFF

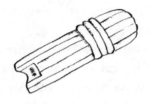

First-class: 9,027 runs (33.80), 350 wickets (31.59) and 185 catches
Tests (79): 3,845 runs (31.77), 226 wickets (32.78) and 52 catches
One-day Internationals (141): 3,394 runs (32.01), 169 wickets
(24.38) and 47 catches

I enjoy hitting the ball and trying to bowl fast, and that is what I do.

Andrew Flintoff

Born in Preston, Lancashire in 1977, between 2004 and 2006 Andrew Flintoff could rightly have laid claim to being the best all-rounder in the game, and one of the best and most intimidating fast bowlers too. His heroic efforts and generous sportsmanship during England's 2005 Ashes victory went a long way to making the series so memorable. But it wasn't always this way for the burly Lancastrian all-rounder. He carried excess weight early in his career, and had to limit his bowling aspirations until his body became strong enough to cope.

After successful England under-19 performances he graduated to the England A Team and, by the summer of 1998 was selected to represent the Test side against South Africa. He fared well in his first Test, but recorded a pair of ducks in his second, and was promptly dropped. He was in and out of both the one-day and Test sides for the next couple of years and it wasn't until the 2001–02 tour to New Zealand that he delivered on his promise, by scoring his maiden Test hundred. In 2003 he had a fantastic series with the bat against South Africa, scoring 423 runs at 52.87. Unfortunately his bowling average was even higher.

Having missed the 2002–03 Ashes series through injury, he seemed eager to show his worth from the very start of the 2005 Ashes series in England. In the space of a few weeks that summer Flintoff became an international superstar. With 402 runs at 40.20 and 24 wickets at 27.79 he took the series by the scruff of the neck and along with his teammates recaptured the Ashes urn for the first time since Gatting's England side were victorious in the 1980s. The nation needed a new cricketing hero, and Flintoff, with his easy northern charm and imposing physical presence, was just the man.

He was selected for the Rest of the World XI to play against Australia and, along with his England teammates, awarded an MBE. In the same year he was named Britain's prestigious Sports Personality of the Year and became *Wisden's* Leading Cricketer in the World for 2005.

Injury had always threatened to overshadow his career, and 2005 was to prove a pinnacle rather than a launch pad to greater feats. He was asked to captain England on their tour to Australia to defend the Ashes in 2006–07, where they were thumped 5–0 in Shane Warne and Glen McGrath's farewell series.

In July 2009, following further debilitating injuries, he announced that he would retire from Test cricket at the end of the Ashes series that summer. Throughout the series he often fought through the pain barrier to bowl England into winning positions, and even ran out Australian captain Ricky Ponting at the Oval to help secure a 2–1 triumph for his side. He retired from professional cricket at the end of the season in 2010 due to ill health.

RESOURCES

WEBSITES

www.espncricinfo.com

www.thecricketer.com

www.guardian.co.uk/sport/cricket

ORGANISATIONS

The England and Wales Cricket Board
www.ecb.co.uk

The International Cricket Council
www.icc-cricket.yahoo.net

The Professional Cricketers' Association
www.thepca.co.uk

PUBLICATIONS

Birley, Derek *A Social History of English Cricket* (Aurum Press, 1999)

Brearley, Mike *The Art of Captaincy* (Hodder & Stoughton, 1985)

Cardus, Neville *Days in the Sun* (Rupert Hart-Davis, 1948)

Fingleton, J. H. *Brightly Fades the Don* (Collins, 1950)

James, C. L. R. *Beyond Boundaries* (Pluto Press, 2006)

Malies, Jeremy *Great Characters from Cricket's Golden Age* (Robson Books, 2000)

Wisden Cricketers' Almanack (annual editions since 1864)

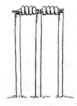

www.summersdale.com